THROWING THINGS AWAY

From Middens to
Resource Recovery

LAURENCE PRINGLE

Thomas Y. Crowell   New York

Photo credits: British Columbia Provincial Museum, 3 (top); Joanna Burger, 44; Canapress Photo Service, 33; City of Riverview, Michigan, 65; Steven J. Krasemann/DRK PHOTO, 37 (bottom); Museum of the City of New York, 8; New York City Department of Sanitation, 10; The New-York Historical Society, 12; Vergil Noble, Midwestern Archeological Research Center and the Museum at Michigan State University, 6; Al Paglione, *The Record*, 64; Portland, Maine, *Press Herald*, 19; Laurence Pringle, iii, 3 (bottom), 20, 24, 27, 31, 35, 37 (top), 40, 41, 43, 48 (top), 52, 54, 56, 58, 61, 63, 68, 70, 72, 77, 81, 83; Saskatchewan Archives Board, 16; Sygma, 29; University of Arizona, 23; Wide World Photos, Inc., 48 (bottom).

Library of Congress Cataloging-in-Publication Data
Pringle, Laurence P.
  Throwing things away.

  Bibliography: p.
  Includes index.
  Summary: Describes the phenomenon of garbage, what it
can indicate about particular cultures, and past and
present problems and methods of solid waste disposal
and management.
  1. Refuse and refuse disposal—Environmental aspects—
Juvenile literature.   2. Litter (Trash)—Environmental
aspects—Juvenile literature.   [1. Refuse and refuse
disposal.   2. Litter (Trash)   I. Title.
TD792.P75 1986   363.7'28   83-46165
ISBN 0-690-04420-8
ISBN 0-690-04421-6 (lib. bdg.)

For Christopher Letts, forager, fisherman, friend

CONTENTS

ONE
A HISTORY BOOK

"Remember to take out the trash, dear," Mother said to her son. He groaned, then reluctantly gathered up the deer bones, oyster shells, and a broken clay pot and carried them from the cave.

From the time of the earliest humans to the present, people have thrown stuff away. We have many names for it: garbage, junk, offal, refuse, rubbish, solid waste, trash, even rejectamenta. Of these, garbage and offal usually refer to organic (once-living) materials. Offal is waste parts from butchered animals. Garbage is left-over or spoiled food, and waste from food preparation.

Most of what we discard decays, but hard objects may last a long time, sometimes for many thousands of years. This material evidence is vital for archeologists, the scientists who study past human life and

1

culture. Like people today, prehistoric humans sometimes had specific places where they threw trash.
These refuse pits might be located in the corner of a
cave, down the rocky slope from a cave entrance, or at
a short distance from a hut or other dwelling. Archeologists call these past dumps for trash "kitchen
middens" or just "middens."

Another type is the "sheet midden"—made up of
objects simply thrown out on the ground surface.
Sometimes the animal bones and other trash of a sheet
midden were gathered up later and put into a natural
or man-made hole in the ground. By then the bones
had been marked by the teeth of dogs, pigs, rodents,
or other mammals that had gnawed on them.

Some middens are located where prehistoric people
camped to feast on some locally abundant food. For
example, along the shores of the Hudson River at Cro-
ton Point, New York, archeologists found a midden of
oyster shells several feet deep and ten acres in size.
Many generations of Indians gathered oysters for food
from the river and discarded the shells. Similar middens, large and small, are found at many other sites
along ocean and estuary coasts of North America.

Besides oyster, clam, and mussel shells, an Indian
midden might contain bones, antlers, nutshells, axes,
and broken or lost tools. Some evidence of past life in
a midden is microscopic in size. Pollen grains, mag-
nified more than a thousand times, can be identified.
They are clues to the past plant life of an area and to

Mounds of castoff clam and oyster shells have been found at the sites of coastal Indian villages. (Drawing made in 1778 at Vancouver Island, British Columbia, Canada.)

Archeologists shake soil through a sifter, leaving oyster shells that were discarded by Native Americans. Spear points and other artifacts are often found in shell middens.

the diet of prehistoric people. They may also reveal how the climate of the past differs from the climate now.

Discarded tools and other artifacts reveal a great deal about the people who used them. In different cultures or tribes, people made weapons, tools, or pots in distinctive ways. Bones and stones were the first materials used for making tools and weapons, long before metalworking was developed. So the material and workmanship of a spear point or other artifact help archeologists determine when and by whom it was made.

The depth of artifacts in the soil can also be an important clue. Some campsites, caves, or other dwelling places were used and abandoned again and again. Each time, the remains of campfires, tools, and other objects were eventually covered with soil. The soil may have been blown in by winds or washed in by water or slowly formed from decaying leaves.

Each abandoned camp or settlement is represented by a sheet midden of discarded objects in a layer of soil that lies above earlier layers, or strata, that also contain artifacts. Thus, items left by the most recent settlers are at or near the surface; those left by the earliest people to use a site are in the deeper layers. The strata are like the pages of a history book. At some sites, archeologists have unearthed layers of artifacts that represent several thousand years of human settlement.

The discovery of artifacts on the surface is often the

first clue that the remains of past peoples lie below. This was the case in the discovery of "lost" Fort Oui-atenon, a French fur trading post on the Wabash River that was built in 1717 near present-day Lafayette, Indiana. Fort Ouiatenon was inhabited by a dozen French fur traders and their families, but by the 1820s no visible trace remained. There was even doubt about which side of the Wabash it had stood upon. In the early 1930s a park with a monument was established where Fort Ouiatenon had supposedly stood, based on the best evidence people could find.

In 1967, however, iron hardware, parts of guns and bottles, and other items from the 1700s were discovered in a cornfield a mile downstream from the park. This was the real fort site, and is still being investigated by archeologists. They have unearthed parts of the stockade's walls, several buildings (including a storehouse littered with trinkets and other trade goods), and refuse pits. From these pits, wells, wall trenches, and sheet middens, archeologists collected thousands of animal bones that had been discarded by the French. Identification of the bones gave some idea of the diet of the people who had lived at the fort. They had relied not on domestic livestock, but on wildlife and fish; the most abundant bones included those of bison, deer, raccoons, wild turkeys, waterfowl (ducks and geese), passenger pigeons, and catfish.

What we today call "solid waste management problems" did not develop until people lived in large per-

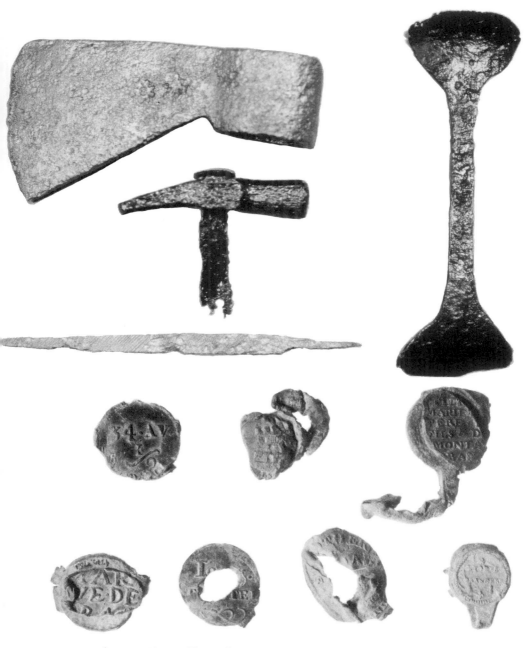

Among the artifacts found where Fort Ouiatenon stood were iron
tools (top) and lead seals (bottom) that had been used to identify
trade goods, such as bundles of blankets.

manent settlements. In Troy and other ancient cities, garbage and other wastes were simply cast into the streets, to the extent that street levels rose and new homes eventually had to be built. Ancient Rome, famed for its advanced system of freshwater aqueducts, failed to cope with its garbage, dead horses, and other wastes produced by more than a million inhabitants. Anyone imagining life during Rome's time of glory, about 2,000 years ago, should include plenty of offensive odors.

The "city dump" had been invented by the Greeks about 500 years earlier. Scavengers in Athens were required to dispose of wastes they collected no less than a mile beyond the city's walls. Athens also tried to halt the throwing of wastes into streets and alleys. But such advances were not widely adopted in the world. Until the fourteenth century, residents of Paris were allowed to throw their garbage out windows. (Now called the airmail method of waste disposal, it is still practiced in some urban neighborhoods.)

The Industrial Revolution, which began in the mid-eighteenth century, caused cities to grow rapidly and become more densely settled. People had more goods to use and discard, but there were no adequate waste-collection and -disposal systems. Befouled and overcrowded, nineteenth-century cities were called "the most degraded urban environment the world had yet seen" by author and social philosopher Lewis Mumford.

Nineteenth-century cities failed to cope with the increasing volumes of solid wastes, which included coal and wood ashes from stoves and furnaces.

Though not an industrial city, Washington, D.C., also suffered from a lack of waste disposal. In his book *Garbage in the Cities*, historian Martin Melosi wrote, "As late as the 1860s, Washingtonians dumped garbage and slop into alleys and streets, pigs roamed freely, slaughterhouses spewed nauseating fumes, and rats and cockroaches infested most dwellings—including the White House."

Nevertheless, progress was being made against indiscriminate dumping, primarily for health reasons. Epidemics of typhoid and other contagious diseases swept through cities, and infant death rates increased. The reason, people thought, was all that smelly garbage, horse manure, and other organic waste. According to the incorrect but then widely accepted miasmic or filth theory of disease, gases from decaying material helped spread diseases.

A minister referred to this notion in his speech at the 1879 meeting of the American Public Health Association, when he described a New Orleans dump: "Thither were brought the dead dogs and cats, the kitchen garbage and the like, and duly dumped. This festering, rotten mess was picked over by rag-pickers and wallowed over by pigs, pigs and humans contesting for a living from it, and as the heaps increased, the odors increased also, and the mass lay corrupting under a tropical sun, dispersing the pestilential fumes where the winds carried them."

People couldn't stop winds from blowing, but they could do something about the garbage and other refuse that lay all about. Dramatic progress was made in collecting solid waste and dumping it on vacant land or into water. In the early 1900s, cities began to estimate or record the amounts and kinds of wastes collected. According to one estimate, each American annually produced from 100 to 180 pounds of garbage (food wastes), 50 to 100 pounds of rubbish, and 300 to 1,200 pounds of wood or coal ashes. People living in

The white uniforms of New York City street cleaners served to remind people that good sanitation protected health.

European cities produced about half as much. Thus, early in this century the United States had already established world leadership in throwing things away.

The turn of the century marked a sort of golden age of sanitation in the United States. New York City street cleaners wore white uniforms. The appearance of White Wings, as they were called, reminded people of doctors, nurses, and others in the health professions. Juvenile Street Cleaning Leagues were established in several cities, including New York, Philadelphia, and Denver. Boys and girls who were members in New York City wore white caps. They voluntarily cleaned up trash and tried to influence others to do the same.

In a letter to the commissioner of New York's Street Cleaning Department, one youngster boasted of tell-ing a man where to dispose of a mattress he had thrown into the street. The man "then picked it up and thanked me for the inflammation I gave him."

The writer's lack of spelling skill was more than equaled by his zeal for cleaning up the city. He reported, "I also picked up 35 banana skins, 43 water mellion shells, 2 bottles, 3 cans, and mattress from Norfolk St."

By the early twentieth century the filth theory of disease had been discarded, replaced by the germ theory—that contagious diseases were caused by bacteria and other microbes. Doctors and other health care workers now understood what they were fighting— and it wasn't foul-smelling gases from garbage. Emphasis was put on the use of inoculations and immunizations to protect people from contagious diseases.

Garbage and other refuse was still seen as a health problem, but certainly not the primary source of disease. The task of collecting and disposing of solid wastes passed from city health departments to public works departments, often directed by engineers. A new profession of sanitary engineer developed. Cities began to have better control of their ever-growing daily output of garbage and other solid wastes.

Collection efforts improved, but disposal of refuse remained a problem. Cities with access to rivers or lakes often dumped wastes into them, but protests and lawsuits from beach resorts and downstream communities curtailed or halted this practice. Some gar-

A dumping ground beside the East River in nineteenth-century New York City.

bage was burned, and some was used as soil fertilizer or pig food. But the primary means of waste disposal was dumping on land, or into marshes or other shallow wetlands. In general, civilization had advanced considerably from the Stone Age, but solid waste disposal had not. At the 1912 convention of the American Public Health Association a doctor said, "In its simplicity and carelessness, as a means of waste disposal, the dump probably dates back to the discarding of the first apple core in the Garden of Eden."

Dumps smelled. Dumps were breeding places for rats. Dump fires smoldered for months. Engineers devised an improvement, the landfill, in which different kinds of solid wastes were arranged in layers. About a foot of garbage was covered with eighteen to twenty-four inches of ashes, street sweepings, or rubbish, followed by another foot of garbage, and so on. Because of the labor involved, this was more expensive than direct dumping of all wastes, but this early landfill method was adopted by several cities in the 1920s.

In 1920 the United States population was 106 million and each person threw away an estimated average 2.75 pounds of solid wastes each day. In 1985, each of 239 million United States residents discarded an average of about 8 pounds a day. This is household trash, and does not include agricultural, mining, and industrial waste. People in the United States are throwing away more stuff than ever before, but the kind of waste has changed and will no doubt continue to change.

Imagine for a moment the discovery of a giant midden where people had dumped solid wastes from the 1920s to the 1980s. Assuming that decay had not destroyed much evidence, what might an archeologist find in the different layers? In the lower strata, until the 1940s, there would be plenty of coal and wood ash. As late as 1939 they made up 43% of New York City's refuse. By the 1960s, however, relatively few people cooked food or heated their homes with coal or wood, so an archeologist would find little ash in recent decades. The layers of trash since 1960 would hold more and more lightweight packaging material—plastic, cardboard, paper—evidence of the throwaway lifestyle of the late-twentieth-century United States.

For a time during the 1950s, before this wasteful life-style took hold, solid wastes seemed well under control. Engineers had developed improved ways of landfilling in which a day's dumped trash was compacted, then covered with a layer of soil. These disposal sites were called sanitary landfills. Though far from sanitary (clean, hygienic) they had fewer rats, fires, and foul smells than earlier landfills or open dumps.

But some modern landfills are now known to leak poisonous chemicals into water supplies. Communities are running out of space to put the stuff that people discard. Mountains of trash rise into the air, and the volume of solid waste continues to grow. So does the cost of collecting, hauling, and covering it. Citizens who never before thought about where their garbage goes are finally beginning to pay attention to the stuff they throw away.

TWO
A CULTURAL
INSTITUTION

Novelist Wallace Stegner spent part of his childhood in the new frontier town of Whitemud, Saskatchewan, Canada, in the early 1900s. For a curious boy there were prairie gulleys and a river edge to explore, but the most fascinating place of all was the town dump. Established by an ordinance of the territorial government, the dump was an official institution before the town was. Unofficially it was also a sort of history book, containing relics of every person who had ever lived in Whitemud, and every phase of the town's brief life.

In an essay called "The Dump Ground" Stegner later wrote of these relics: "The bedsprings on which Whitemud's first child was begotten might be out there; the skeleton of a boy's pet colt; books soaked

15

A frontier town in Saskatchewan, Canada, similar to Wallace Stegner's boyhood home of Whitemud.

with water and chemicals in a house fire, and thrown out to flap their stained eloquence in the prairie wind."

Children prowled among the broken dishes, rusty barbed wire, smashed wagon wheels, and cast-off furniture, looking for such marketable items as lead, tinfoil, and bottles. Sometimes they uncovered a piece of lead casing that had enclosed the wires of the town's first telephone system. The soft lead was just the right size for rings. Children carved initials or pierced hearts in the lead rings. "They served a purpose in juvenile courtship," Stegner recalled, "but they stopped a good way short of art."

"Most of our gleanings," Stegner continued, "we left lying around barn or attic or cellar until in some renewed fury of spring cleanup our families carted them off to the dump again, to be rescued and briefly treasured by some other boy. Occasionally something we really valued with a passion was snatched from us in horror and returned at once. That happened to the mounted head of a white mountain goat, somebody's trophy from old times and the far Rocky Mountains, that I brought home one day. My mother took one look and discovered that his beard was full of moths."

Looking back at his childhood, Stegner realized why the dump so fascinated the children of Whitemud: "This was the kitchen midden of all the civilization we knew. It gave us the most tantalizing glimpses into our neighbors' lives and our own. . . . I think I learned more from the Town Dump than I learned from school; more about people, more about how life is lived, not elsewhere but there, not in other times but now."

Today Wallace Stegner's boyhood experiences seem exotic to millions of people who do not even know where their trash is taken. But small-town dumps and landfills of the United States and Canada still retain some of the flavor of Whitemud's dump. For more than twenty years the town of Kennebunkport, Maine, has held a dump festival, "to honor the old-fashioned town dump, a fast-disappearing segment of Americana." Each July a dozen or more young women search through trash in Kennebunkport to find something to wear in the Miss Dumpy contest. The goal is to be as repugnant as possible, so costumes often feature beer cans, grapefruit rinds, and large dead fish.

There are thousands of dumps and landfills across the United States and Canada where trash is still brought by individuals and families, who unload their own car trunks, station wagons, or pickup trucks. The vehicles do not always leave empty—something of real or imagined value is often carried home. At some sites an area is established where people set aside items they believe others might want. The town dump may be jokingly called "the exchange."

In Truro, Massachusetts, on Cape Cod, residents telephone Richard Steele, manager of the dump, and ask him to watch out for certain items they want. When the object comes to the dump, he sets it aside for the caller. Richard Steele is always alert for items people can use. He repairs some himself or gives dump "customers" advice on how to fix them. Within or near the dump's shack lie lawn chairs, lawn mowers, water skis, television sets, lumber, fencing, stuffed animals, bicycles, and toys—all free to any town resident who can use them.

On a recent June morning Richard Steele said that since Christmas he had given fifteen bicycles from the dump to Truro children. "I hate to see useful objects

Winner of the 1984 Miss Dumpy contest (right) in the annual dump celebration held in Kennebunkport, Maine.

Richard Steele encourages people to salvage useful items from the trash others have brought to the dump in Truro, Massachusetts.

smashed by the bulldozer," he said. He laments that so much refuse now comes to the dump sealed in plastic bags, in which many valuable objects can't be spotted and rescued. But he also notes that people are more aware of the value of such items as antiques and collectibles, which are now more likely to be offered at yard sales or flea markets than brought to the dump.

"Picking," or scavenging for valuables, is permitted at some dumps and landfills. A fee may be charged for the privilege. Scavengers watch for the most readily marketable materials, such as aluminum, and also for appliances and other items that can be repaired and used or sold. Often no repair is needed; many discarded items are in good working order.

Dump pickers are always alert for purses, and search the pockets of clothing, for they have learned that people throw away lots of money. The amounts are usually small, but a landfill employee in New York State found $450 in trash discarded by a store.

All sorts of valuable things are buried in dumps and landfills. In 1985, Craig Claiborne, food editor of *The New York Times*, wrote of a great treasure he was given —several white truffles from Italy. Although these fungi give off an intense, acrid smell, white truffles have an extraordinary flavor and are worth even more than black truffles. Claiborne decided to save them for a special feast, and stored them in a plastic container in the refrigerator. While he was away, the cleaning lady came. As she told him later, "I never knew things could stink so. I threw those things in the East Hampton dump." Thus some of the most expensive delicacies on earth were probably eaten by gulls.

Sometimes people realize they have accidentally thrown away something valuable and try to retrieve it. Managers of every dump and landfill have stories to tell about a wedding ring, a $4,000 mink coat, or valuable papers that were thrown into the trash by accident. Some of the stories have happy endings, but many do not. Sixty thousand dollars worth of aircraft parts were mistakenly buried in a New York State landfill. Two weeks of digging with a backhoe failed to unearth them.

The chances of recovering valuables from the trash are good if the loss is discovered quickly and the sanitation department is notified. Often the specific garbage truck can be identified and halted when it reaches the landfill. Then its contents are dumped in a separate area where they can be searched. According to landfill employees, each year such valuable objects as jewelry and money are recovered in this way.

In 1962 Wallace Stegner wrote, "If I were a sociologist anxious to study in detail the life of any community I would go very early to its refuse piles." A decade later this is exactly what anthropologist William L. Rathje of the University of Arizona began to do. He said, "Archeologists have long used refuse from ancient cultures to reconstruct behavior; modern household garbage is no less a reflection of the behavior of those who have generated it."

Dr. Rathje and his students began to study Tucson's garbage in the early 1970s. With the cooperation of the city's sanitation department, they compared garbage collected from well-to-do neighborhoods with that from poorer areas. As the study expanded, supported by grants from the U.S. Environmental Protection Agency (EPA) and the National Science Foundation, researchers were able to investigate the garbage from more homes, taking a larger sample of the city's population.

Taking part in a long-term study, University of Arizona students analyze garbage collected from different Tucson neighborhoods.

Students usually wear lab coats, rubber gloves, and surgical masks as they sort through bags of garbage that have been collected from different areas of Tucson and set aside by sanitation workers. Anything of a personal nature is discarded to prevent invasion of privacy. A lot can be learned about an individual or an institution by sorting through items that have been thrown away. That's why some celebrities guard against people snooping in their trash, and paper shredders are used to protect information in some businesses and government agencies.

According to Dr. Rathje, the study reveals that Tuc-

No two loads of trash are alike, and solid wastes also vary with the seasons, with economic conditions, and with localities.

son's residents throw away 15% of their edible food, at an annual cost of $11 to $13 million. Most of this is not in tiny bits but in large, usable amounts, such as whole steaks and half-used packages of soup. Comparing different neighborhoods, the study showed that middle-income people wasted more food (and usable tools and appliances) than the poor or rich. People in low-income neighborhoods bought the most costly educational toys for children.

Interviews with people in their homes, compared with actual evidence from garbage collected from their neighborhoods, revealed that people throw away much more edible food than they like to admit. They also don't like to tell survey takers how much beer they drink. People claimed their beer consumption was about one eighth of that actually documented from the trash of their neighborhood.

Garbage research—garbageology—has spread to other cities and nations, and has had some practical effects in schools and homes. For example, after a study of its garbage, a fraternity house at the University of Southern California was able to cut its food costs by about a thousand dollars a year by eliminating certain foods entirely and by reducing the serving sizes of others.

Dr. Rathje continues to investigate Tucson's garbage. In the magazine *Science 81* he explained the importance of this garbage-can archeology: "So much of our culture is being demolished so fast that we have to start digging before it's too late. Our practice of ripping buildings down to the foundations and carting off the rubble means future archeologists aren't going to find useful ruins. . . . It's the same with cultural artifacts. Everything ends up in a dump where it gets bulldozed, mixed up, and crushed. Stratigraphic layers won't be available for analysis."

In an informal way people who collect garbage and who work at landfills observe cultural changes too. During a recession in 1972, New York City landfills received only about a tenth of the normal amounts of rubble from buildings being torn down for new construction. The amount of garbage and other waste also declined, as people threw away less food and had appliances repaired rather than discard them. More recently, the establishment of beverage-container deposit laws in several states has reduced the volume of bottles and cans brought to dumps and landfills.

New products are marketed, a game or toy becomes a national fad, and soon landfill workers see the first wave of discards. When color television became affordable for most families, great numbers of black-and-white sets were thrown away. A department store holds a sale on mattresses, and the waste stream flowing to the dump contains a brief spate of worn mattresses.

The seasons also bring change. Spring and fall cleaning increase the volume of material, especially of branches and leaves from trees and shrubs, and other garden or yard debris. In northern states many people put snow tires on their autos in the late autumn. They throw away worn tires in great numbers at that time. After Christmas there is an increase in wrapping paper, broken toys, and also many toys in perfect working order. (People also accidentally throw away a lot of gift checks and cash at that time.) In a college town the volume of waste drops sharply during summer vacation, while summer is the time of peak trash volume at northern shore resorts.

Solid wastes are as diverse as the people who produce them. No two loads of trash are alike, no two days of trash are alike, and no two towns are alike in their refuse. Every landfill receives occasional odd, memorable items to bury. A twenty-five–by–forty-foot houseboat was interred at the Dallas, Texas, landfill. A killer whale that died at the Miami

Solid wastes in the United States include many still functional or repairable tools, appliances, and other useful items.

Seaquarium was buried in the Dade County landfill. In the same landfill are the remains of a remarkable artwork. In May 1983 the artist Christo, with 430 helpers, created "Surrounded Islands"—surrounding eleven small islands in Miami's Biscayne Bay with floating skirts of bright-pink plastic fabric. After two weeks the artwork was dismantled, and 6.5 million square feet of polypropylene went to the landfill.

The endless variety of stuff that arrives at landfills makes them fascinating places to work. But landfill workers are often appalled at the waste they see— food, many functional tools and appliances, a truckload of irregular but usable shoes. Wallace Stegner's words come to mind: "A community may be as well judged by what it throws away—what it has to throw away and what it chooses to—as by any other evidence."

According to an agency of the United Nations, in many Third World cities "1 to 2 percent of the population is supported directly or indirectly by refuse from the upper 10 to 20 percent." Scavenging at a city dump is often the first "employment" of poor peasants who have emigrated from rural areas. In Mexico City thousands of people pay dues to a scavenger's union, in order to hunt for goods in the city's huge dump. In Colombo, the capital of Sri Lanka, people wait for the garbage trucks to reach the dumps, then rush forward to search for items of value. After

Scavengers eke out a meager living by picking metal cans from the dump at Manila in the Philippines.

the people leave, cows forage in the garbage. They are followed by pigs and goats. Last are the crows.

For these people and many others in developing nations, the dumps and landfills of the United States and Canada might seem like pieces of heaven on earth.

THREE
A FEAST
FOR WILDLIFE

The last garbage truck drove off and the dump was closed. Dusk deepened into night. Then sounds came from amid the cans, boxes, and other clutter—scurrying, scratching, and squeaking sounds. If you suddenly flashed a searchlight over the dump, you would see the glowing eyes and scuttling forms of many rats.

Norway rats thrive in the abundant food and shelter of a dump environment. When part of a dump burns, workers tell of hordes of rats racing from their hideouts. In some communities, rat shooting at the town dump is still a form of nighttime recreation.

At landfills, however, rats are usually scarce. Workers see them arrive—leaping from trucks or newly dumped trash—but a well-managed landfill is not a good rat habitat. Not only is garbage covered with soil

30

Vultures wheel in the sky over a landfill south of Miami, Florida.

daily, but it and the soil are compacted by heavy equipment, so that rats cannot usually establish a stable network of tunnels and dens in which to hide and reproduce. Occasional use of poisons keeps the numbers of both rats and mice low.

These rodents are only a few of the animal species that are attracted to the abundant food at dumps and landfills. Many wild mammals and birds depend on the garbage discarded by people. The animal species vary from region to region. At southern and southwestern dumps and landfills, wild pigs and vultures are common scavengers at some waste disposal sites. Vultures normally eat carrion (dead animals) and find bits of meat at landfills. According to an observer at the Dade County, Florida, landfill, when the carcass of a dog or other large mammal is left exposed on the surface, vultures pick its bones clean in a few hours.

Far to the north, polar bears scavenge at dumps in Churchill, Manitoba, on the western coast of Canada's Hudson Bay. Churchill lies in the path of polar-bear seasonal travels. When the bay ice breaks up, usually in July, more than 1,000 bears come ashore about 200 miles south of Churchill, near the Manitoba-Ontario border. They spend the summer there, eating very little, and the adult females nurse their cubs in dens. In the fall the bears head north toward Cape Churchill on the coast, waiting for the formation of ice on the bay, which will enable them to catch and eat the seals that are their main food.

About 200 polar bears come to Churchill itself, looking for food to tide them over until the ice forms. They congregate at the dump. The bears are a mixed blessing for Churchill. They attract tourists, who are delighted to snap pictures of the mature 1,000-pound adults. The bears are also a menacing nuisance, sometimes seeking food from inside homes. A man was killed in 1983 and others have been mauled by bears; everyone is cautious outdoors during the annual bear invasion. Stores sell sweat shirts that say, "Our household pests are polar bears."

Biologists have tagged individual bears to study their travels. Some bears captured in town and airlifted 300 to 400 miles away returned to the Churchill dump within a few weeks, apparently by swimming long distances in Hudson Bay.

Other kinds of bears are also attracted to the easily

32

Polar bears are both a nuisance and a major tourist attraction in Churchill, Manitoba, where they sometimes forage at the dump.

obtained food at dumps and landfills. Throughout their range, black bears forage at night in rural dumps. People armed with flashlights and cameras come to see them. The bears feed quietly, undisturbed by their observers. They seem too placid to some foolish people, who throw objects at them in order to get more exciting photographs. To the black bears' credit, they rarely hurt people.

Grizzly bears are another matter; they sometimes kill humans. Dumps have played a role in bringing these bears and people into contact. Hotels established within the boundaries of some western national parks were allowed to dump their garbage nearby. Some hotel managers deliberately put food scraps close to their buildings, to attract wildlife for the amusement of guests. These "bears at the dump" shows were major attractions, but some park officials warned that trouble lay ahead.

One August night in 1967, grizzly bears killed two women in Glacier National Park. One victim died near the Granite Park Chalet, where grizzlies had been lured with garbage. In 1980, two of three people killed by grizzlies in the same park were mauled by a bear that had frequented a dump just outside the park border. They unwittingly camped where the bear was most likely to travel between the dump and the park. Dumps within Glacier and Yellowstone national parks have been closed, but those located nearby still lure grizzlies, and tend to make these dangerous bears less wary of humans.

In northern Minnesota, biologist Holly Hertel saw black bears at a dump being harassed by timber wolves. She studied a specific wolf pack, called the Perch Lake pack, from 1981 to 1983. Members of the pack were known to frequent a local dump, so part of her research involved watching at night from an observation blind, equipped with a spotlight. Using a night vision scope, she was able to identify individual members of the wolf pack, most of which she had earlier trapped and marked in distinctive ways before releasing them.

In spring and early summer the wolf pack stayed near dens where pups were raised. Then, in July, some of the wolves began to forage at the dump. They arrived about midnight and stayed as late as seven A.M.

The Perch Lake wolf pack killed relatively few deer in the wintertime, relying on food from a dump instead.

Black bears also fed at the dump, from about nine P.M. until two A.M. At times several wolves and as many as ten bears were within Holly Hertel's view.

The bears and wolves usually stayed at least fifteen feet apart. Sometimes a bear stepped toward a wolf, forcing it to give up some food. More often, a wolf tried to make a bear move, though this was seldom successful. A wolf would step closer and closer to a bear, invading its "personal space." This harassment seldom caused a bear to give up its food. Wolves were more successful when they boldly charged and chased bears.

About the end of September, bears stopped visiting the dump and soon hibernated in their dens. Wolves continued to seek food there. The pack killed relatively few deer in the wintertime—evidence that they were finding vital food at the dump. Holly Hertel concluded that the artificial food supply at the dump had another effect on the Perch Lake pack: it enabled the wolves to have a smaller-than-usual territory. Ordinarily a pack of six to eight wolves that eats only natural prey must maintain a territory larger than the thirty-one square miles occupied by the Perch Lake pack.

In more settled areas, packs of feral dogs—abandoned or runaway pets gone wild—often scavenge for food at dumps and landfills. Some people deliberately abandon their pets at landfills, perhaps in the hope that the animals will somehow scratch a living from the garbage. Cats have a better chance of survival than dogs; they need less food and can more easily find shelter in piles of tree stumps, furniture, and "white goods" (old refrigerators, washers, and dryers). At the Denver-Arapahoe County landfill, east of Denver, Colorado, some feral cats lived in a huge collection of car, truck, and tractor tires.

Raccoons and opossums, wild mammals that eat both animal and plant matter (omnivores), are also attracted to dumps and landfills. Such birds as crows, ravens, vultures, starlings, and gulls are similarly drawn to the plentiful food. Bald eagles pick through the garbage of some Alaskan dumps, with the best-known gathering located on Adak Island in the Aleutians. Adak is the site of a United States Navy base and weather station, and a home for about 5,000 people.

Animals may find shelter in unburied waste. Wild housecats once lived among several million tires at the Denver-Arapahoe County landfill.

Bald eagles scrounge for food at the dump on Adak Island in the Aleutians (Stephen J. Krasemann/DRK PHOTO).

Their refuse, including plenty of food scraps, lures nearly a hundred bald eagles as well as many ravens and gulls to the Adak landfill.

Some people are disturbed by this situation: the bald eagle, majestic white-headed symbol of the United States, dining in a dump. Others feel that the relationship is an apt one: a dump or landfill reveals much of a nation's culture and values, and just as surely as that's "our" eagle, that's one of our dumps.

In the warmer months the bald eagles find plenty of fish and carrion, but they rely heavily on the landfill during the winter. This artificial food supply enables the Adak Island region to support an unusually high year-round eagle population.

In wintertime, great numbers of migratory birds feed on landfills in the southern United States. For example, in February 1980 nine species totaling about 15,000 birds were seen foraging at a landfill in Deerfield Beach, Broward County, Florida. They included turkey vultures, cattle egrets, three species of gulls, and four kinds of perching birds (starlings, red-winged blackbirds, boat-tailed grackles, and brown-headed cowbirds). The behavior of different species was observed by Joanna Burger of Rutgers University and Michael Gochfeld of the Rutgers Medical School. They found that the vultures, herring gulls, and perching birds waited nearby while bulldozers moved garbage around. All but the vultures flew in to feed whenever the bulldozers stopped, if only for a few minutes. The vultures stayed away until all operations ceased for the day.

When bulldozers were active, ring-billed gulls fed on garbage but kept a safe distance and fled quickly when one of the big machines approached. Laughing gulls and cattle egrets seemed most comfortable grabbing bits of food near operating bulldozers. The egrets were especially unafraid of the big machines—they did not fly until a bulldozer was very close, and then flew only a short distance. They are called cattle egrets because they normally feed close to grazing livestock, so to them a bulldozer may seem like an especially large and noisy cow.

People usually associate gulls with landfills, but some gull species rarely visit dumps. The small Bonaparte's gull, for example, snatches fish and other prey from the water's surface of lakes or along ocean coasts. The gull species at landfills are mostly large species that are opportunistic ground feeders. In eastern North America these are herring gulls, ring-billed gulls, and great black-backed gulls. On the West Coast the common gulls at landfills include herring and ring-billed gulls, plus the California gull, western gull, and glaucous-winged gull.

The number of gulls at a landfill usually varies with the season. In the wintertime an estimated 100,000 herring and ring-billed gulls gather at the vast Fresh Kills landfill on Staten Island, New York. These gulls disperse to other landfills or to beach nesting areas in

Gulls rest on flat, open areas at or near landfills.

the summer. In their normal daily routine, gulls also leave landfills and fly to safe nighttime roosting areas—bodies of water, islands, or beaches. At sunrise they fly back to landfills or to open, flat loafing sites nearby. About three hours before sunset they fly back to their roosting sites. The distance that gulls fly daily between landfill and roosting site is often eighty or more miles during their nesting period and substantially farther during the fall and winter.

Gulls are intelligent, adaptable birds, and fit their activity patterns to the daily and weekly routines of garbage dumping. If dumping is restricted to week-

They spring into action when garbage is dumped and spread.

days, the gulls head for the beach or elsewhere on weekends. René Bollengier, biologist for the U.S. Fish and Wildlife Service, observed how gulls adapted to the schedule of refuse collection and dumping in Manchester, New Hampshire.

Each weekday morning trucks of various colors bring trash from businesses to Manchester's landfill. The gulls, mostly herring gulls and usually several thousand strong, wait quietly on the ground and pay little attention. Experience has taught them that there is little food on those early trucks. Then, at about ten A.M., the gulls begin to fidget in anticipation. Soon the city's orange sanitation trucks, loaded with household garbage, begin to appear. Swarms of gulls descend where garbage is disgorged.

A few herring gulls are so intent on grabbing chunks of food that they are injured or even killed by the wheels of machines used to compact the garbage. Large gulls can continue feeding even after a day's garbage is covered with soil. At the Manchester landfill, herring gulls peck and scratch through several inches of sand, and pull on plastic bags in order to reach morsels of food.

In New Jersey, biologist Joanna Burger studied the landfill feeding behavior of two gull species—herring gulls and laughing gulls. The latter were once rare at landfills. Beginning about 1975, however, their numbers began to increase at New Jersey landfills. Joanna Burger discovered a likely reason for this change by observing the gulls at the Edgeboro landfill in New Brunswick, New Jersey.

She found that the larger herring gulls were the dominant species. A laughing gull hovering over the dump could not displace a herring gull already feeding on the ground, but a herring gull could always displace a feeding laughing gull. Joanna Burger concluded that "Laughing Gulls of all ages move over, depart, or never land in the presence of Herring Gulls."

This may seem like a hopeless situation for the laughing gulls, but they still managed to get food. The

The large herring gulls are able to scratch through soil and tear open bags in order to uncover food.

herring gulls foraged over the entire dump surface; they always landed to feed, and their size and strength enabled them to turn over objects and break open bags. In contrast, laughing gulls foraged where garbage was being dumped, bulldozed around, and compacted. They landed to feed when possible, but could also hover and dip for food items, successfully grabbing morsels while heavy machinery roared and clanked over the active face of the landfill. Having snatched some food, the laughing gulls usually flew off to land and eat it. Some food was pirated by herring gulls, but the laughing gulls ate well enough.

Joanna Burger believes that the change from open dumps to landfills in New Jersey has enabled laughing gulls to compete successfully with herring gulls. In the past, garbage lay uncovered for long periods, and

Laughing gulls fly close to the machines that spread and compact garbage. They may land to feed but also dip down, grab a morsel, and fly off to eat it.

the big herring gulls picked away at will. At today's landfills, however, food is covered with soil but is available while bulldozers break bags open and food spills out. The agile laughing gulls are better able to exploit this situation than herring gulls. As a result, Joanna Burger predicts laughing gulls may increase their use of landfills, and increase their populations as well.

There's no doubt that other gull species have increased in numbers as a result of food available at dumps and landfills. The abundant year-round food increases the survival of chicks and juveniles in the breeding season, and of both young and adult in the wintertime. This caused problems near landfills and also far away, where the gulls nest. At nesting areas along ocean coasts and Great Lakes shores, gulls have displaced terns, causing tern numbers to drop sharply.

The Manchester, New Hampshire, landfill is about a quarter mile from a complex of industrial buildings. Gulls nesting on the forty or so acres of their flat rooftops have created a sanitation problem near ventilation systems. Heavy use by gulls of a nearby reservoir used for human drinking water also presents a potential health problem. Perhaps, it was suggested, these problems would be solved by reducing the number of gulls at the landfill. Before this was tried, however, biologist René Bollengier sought to find out more about the gull population and gull movements at the landfill.

He and several helpers caught 145 herring gulls during the nesting season. The birds were sprayed with a red dye, then released. Bird-watching groups and other observers were alerted to watch for these color-marked birds.

Most of the sightings were within a radius of eighty-three miles, but marked gulls were spotted in New Jersey, Virginia, and forty miles at sea. Another batch of gulls was marked in November, during fall migration. Within twenty-four hours, seven red-dyed gulls were sighted on Long Island, New York, about 170 miles—as the gull flies—from Manchester.

Landfill gulls, René Bollengier learned, are highly mobile. The numbers of birds at the Manchester landfill ranged from 15,000 in the fall to less than 200 in the summer. He noticed big changes during a single day, with mostly adults present at one time, mostly young present at other times. From these observations and from sighting reports of dye-marked gulls, he concluded that landfills provide gulls with "a string of grocery stores. They don't stay in one spot. They hit one place and move on to the next as their schedule or the dumping schedule dictates." Or, as a newspaper headline put it: "Seagulls Tour Landfills to Sample Local Cuisine."

Finding ways to reduce gull numbers, or to keep them away from certain landfills, has been the goal of many studies. Besides fouling the environment with their droppings, gulls pose other problems. In the Great Lakes region, booming populations of ring-billed gulls sometimes eat tomatoes, corn, strawberries, and other farm crops. Gulls also represent a risk of collisions with aircraft. Many kinds of birds, including geese, hawks, vultures, and even flocks of starlings, may collide with airplanes, but gulls are the number-one hazard to aircraft worldwide.

Landfills are often located within a few miles of airports and are sometimes much closer. Gulls may use runways as resting places or fly over airports while commuting between landfills and roosting sites. Furthermore, although gulls commonly fly below altitudes of 800 feet, they may ride updrafts of warm air (thermals) to 3,000 feet or higher. Entire flocks of several thousand gulls may soar over a landfill—a potential hazard to aircraft.

In 1975, a jet airliner taking off from New York's Kennedy Airport with 129 passengers aboard sucked 27 gulls into one engine. The engine exploded and set the aircraft on fire. The passengers and crew managed to escape with only a few injuries. A large landfill beneath the airport's flight path was subsequently closed. Gulls also caused two small planes to crash, in 1977 and 1979, with a total of six fatalities. Each year brings several dozen less-serious gull-aircraft collisions. Damage to commercial airplanes in the United States has been estimated at several million dollars a year.

The danger of gull crashes with private, commercial, and military airplanes led to research aimed to minimize damage to jet engines and airplane windshields. Dead gulls were fired by cannons at speeds up to 500 miles per hour into engines and against windshields. At that speed a two-pound gull hits with a force of 20 tons. These simulations of flying airplanes meeting flying gulls have helped engineers better protect aircraft from real meetings in the air.

Gulls and other birds still pose a hazard, however, and pilots are made aware of bird collisions in their

Gulls sometimes soar several thousand feet above landfills and pose a hazard to low-flying aircraft.

The remains of a jet airliner felled by gulls in 1975.

training. Firecrackers, recorded distress calls, and even live hawks are used to drive gulls off runways. Beginning in 1974, the Federal Aviation Administration (FAA) advised that no landfills should be located within 10,000 feet of a runway used by jet aircraft, or within 5,000 feet of a runway used by propeller-driven airplanes. These standards are in force at FAA-controlled airports and have been adopted by many states with smaller airports.

In the long run, one way to reduce the problems posed by gull populations is to locate new landfills at sites that do not appeal to these birds. Few gulls are attracted to a landfill that lacks large, flat loafing areas, is well away from water, and is surrounded by trees. For existing landfills, in extreme cases garbage can be dumped and covered at night, making the area less attractive to day-feeding gulls.

Landfill operators in Los Angeles County, California, have found a way to discourage large populations of gulls from scavenging. Their system involves setting up forty-foot-tall metal poles on stands, spaced fifty to one hundred feet apart, with steel or monofilament fishing line strung between the poles. A network of these poles is set up around the area where garbage is being dumped and buried. The flight pattern of descending gulls is interrupted by wires or line strung above the garbage, and they veer off.

This method is not foolproof—some gulls land beyond the protected area and walk in under the wires.

Overall, however, the number of gulls present at Los Angeles County landfills has decreased. In one small canyon where the elevated lines covered the entire disposal area, gulls were not able to reach the ground. A few days after the system was installed, the entire gull population left and did not return.

Another method of repelling gulls was tried in the early 1980s. Within six months of opening in 1982, a new landfill near the Massachusetts coast had attracted a population of 3,000 gulls, whose droppings were a nuisance to a nearby residential neighborhood. In May 1983, twenty-four pieces of bread containing a chemical repellant called Avitrol were scattered at the landfill. Gulls that ate the bread flew erratically and gave distress calls. Some died, but the distress calls frightened other gulls off. Thus the death of a few birds was sufficient to keep thousands away. (As migratory birds, gulls are protected by federal law, so special permission must be obtained to kill them.)

Gulls have appeared again at the landfill, but occasional use of Avitrol keeps their numbers low. In ways like this, gulls can be discouraged from gathering in large numbers at landfills where they are a nuisance or a potential threat to aircraft. Of course, they may move on to feed at other landfills or dumps. As long as people continue to dispose of edible food in this way, gulls and many other wild animals will be attracted and will prosper.

50

FOUR
OVERFLOWING LANDFILLS

Cities built on coastal plains or other flat land usually have no low places to fill with trash. Faced with this problem, in 1967 the city of Virginia Beach, Virginia, began to pile refuse higher and higher. In five years the city's waste had become a mountainous ridge, officially named Mount Trashmore. Composed of 400,000 tons of solid waste and 280,000 tons of soil, Mount Trashmore stands sixty feet above the surrounding landscape.

Closed as a landfill and used for recreation, grass-covered Mount Trashmore Park drew a lot of media attention in the early 1970s. However, it was soon dwarfed by successors. Virginia Beach itself is creating another mountain of waste that will be 150 feet tall in the year 2015. That height has already been exceeded by landfills in New Jersey.

51

Mount Trashmore, in Virginia Beach, Virginia, was among the first "mountains" of waste to become a recreation area.

The world's largest landfill is located on the western edge of Staten Island, the least developed of New York City's five boroughs. The landfill lies on both sides of a creek called Fresh Kills. (The word "kill" comes from the original Dutch settlers' term for "channel.") Once a place of woods, ponds, and marshes, the Fresh Kills area became a dumping ground in the 1940s. The City of New York gradually acquired 3,000 acres of the area, of which 2,000 acres is suitable for dumping. As the city's other landfills have been closed, greater and greater amounts of refuse are brought to Fresh Kills.

Six days a week, twenty-four hours a day, barges deliver at least 10,000 tons of solid wastes daily to Fresh Kills. Giant steel jaws suspended from cranes take ten-cubic-yard bites from the barges and drop the waste into wagons. Then tractors pull pairs of these wagons over garbage plains and slopes, to the currently active dumping area. Fresh Kills had two peaks about 160 feet high in 1985. By the year 2000 they could tower 500 feet in the air—easily the highest land along the eastern seaboard.

Although called a landfill, the Fresh Kills facility stretches the meaning of the term because refuse is often left without soil cover for several days. Then it is an open dump, providing a rich smorgasbord for gulls. Winds carry lightweight paper and plastic litter beyond the landfill's borders, and foul odors drift to nearby residential areas.

If one thing distinguishes landfills from dumps, it is the six inches of soil used to cover a layer of compacted refuse at the end of each day. Cover soil reduces odors, wind-blown litter, and water seepage through the wastes. It helps prevent the spread of disease organisms. Fresh Kills is not unique in its failure to cover refuse properly. There are still many more dumps than landfills in the United States, primarily because direct dumping is a much cheaper way to get rid of solid wastes than maintaining a landfill at recommended standards.

Obtaining and transporting soil cover can be expen-

At Fresh Kills, cranes transfer wastes from barges to large wagons (left). Tractors then haul pairs of the wagons (right) up the landfill slopes to be dumped.

sive, although some communities have no trouble getting soil at little or no cost from their landfill sites, from highway departments, or from building contractors. One town may provide cover soil to another in exchange for reduced dumping fees at its landfill. A Florida landfill in need of cover arranged to get it from a nearby housing development. Sarasota County agreed to dig several lakes, ranging from ten to fifty acres in size, for the development. From these excavations the county acquired more than a million cubic yards of soil, which extended the life of its Bee Ridge landfill for another fifteen years.

Even when it has adequate soil cover, the Fresh Kills landfill causes troublesome environmental problems. It borders directly on the Arthur Kill, a channel that separates Staten Island and New Jersey. From the landfill, tidal currents carry buoyant refuse up and down the shore of Staten Island and across to New Jersey. Some of it washes onto the beaches of New Jersey communities, including Woodbridge Township, eight miles south of Fresh Kills. Pieces of wood, tires, bottles, disposable diapers, and even hospital waste litter the beaches, especially after storms or winds from the east. The hospital refuse includes bags of hypodermic needles and infectious materials that have been illegally dumped at Fresh Kills.

In 1979 the township sued New York City, attempting to have the huge dump shut down. Instead, a judge ordered the city to take steps to keep refuse from falling or blowing into the Arthur Kill. A specially designed boat patrols the barge-unloading area, scooping debris from the water. Floating barriers called booms also prevent some trash from escaping. But the booms must be opened to allow barges to pass in and out of Fresh Kills. When this occurs, an outgoing tide sweeps floating wastes into the Arthur Kill and to New Jersey beaches.

In 1982 a judge ordered New York City to pay the salaries of four people whose sole job is cleaning refuse

A sweeper boat scoops spilled trash from the water, then returns it to barges in an effort to keep wastes from reaching communities near Fresh Kills.

from the beaches of Woodbridge Township. Nevertheless, a town beach had to be closed because of the health hazard from floating waste. Although the courts are not about to close New York City's main landfill, they are likely to order the city to take whatever steps are needed to halt this gross pollution.

Like many landfills, Fresh Kills produces a liquid waste called leachate. It forms when rainwater or melted snow passes through solid wastes, picking up organic and inorganic matter. Although small in quantity, leachate may contain highly concentrated pollutants. At Fresh Kills, analyses found small amounts of arsenic, polychlorinated biphenyls (PCBs), heavy metals, and other toxic substances in leachate. It seeps into the Arthur Kill and has reached the natural underground water storage zone (aquifer) of the area; however, so far no leachate has been detected in any well water drawn from the aquifer.

Every landfill and dump is a potential water polluter. Most are located either in wetlands, on flood plains, or over aquifers. According to a 1980 study by the Environmental Protection Agency, 90% of the landfills in the eastern United States leak toxic substances into groundwater. (Conditions are somewhat better in the arid West because there is much less precipitation.)

The EPA estimate did not include disposal sites where toxic wastes were once dumped legally, such as the Love Canal site in Niagara Falls, New York. The study referred to ordinary landfills, where the dumping of hazardous wastes is forbidden.

In Jackson Township, New Jersey, pollution from a community landfill forced more than 160 families to abandon their wells and have water trucked to their homes. Tests showed that tap water in a four-square-mile area contained chloroform, benzene, toluene, mercury, and ingredients found in industrial solvents and insecticides. The source: an underground "cloud" of leachate that began at the town landfill. A court order closed the dump in 1980.

57

Water soaking into buried wastes picks up pollutants. This liquid, called leachate, may contaminate nearby water supplies.

Nearby residents claimed that their contaminated water had caused skin rashes, liver ailments, kidney failures, and other health problems. In 1983 they sued the town for damages. Jackson Township claimed it had not knowingly allowed toxic wastes to be dumped, but a jury concluded that the town had been negligent. The families were awarded more than $17 million in compensation—for the costs of being linked to a new water system, for emotional distress, and for a medical fund to test for cancer and other diseases that might develop later as a result of their use of the polluted water.

Whether public or private, many landfills once received some toxic wastes, which are supposed to be put in specially designed landfills or disposed of in other ways. More stringent federal and state laws now keep most toxic wastes from landfills. At Los Angeles County landfills, full-time health inspectors choose trucks at random and examine their loads. They and the bulldozer operators also check for hazardous materials where refuse is dumped. Suspicious-looking containers are investigated, and the California State Department of Health can take legal action against those who try to sneak hazardous materials into landfills.

Lax enforcement of state laws and landfill regulations still allows some dumping of toxic wastes. In 1986 the New York State Attorney General announced the results of an investigation at thirty-four different landfills in New York. Undercover agents drove vans into the landfills and tried to dump a liquid from fifty-five-gallon drums—the type of container that often holds toxic wastes. The drums held plain water, but if they had held dangerous waste, it could have been dumped at twenty-nine landfills. The agents were stopped and turned away at just five disposal sites.

Even without drums of toxic wastes, however, a landfill can contaminate groundwater with hazardous chemicals. Ordinary household trash includes containers of pesticides, paints, paint thinners, varnishes, cleaning agents (drain cleaners, disinfectants, degreasers), and automotive products (waste oil, antifreeze, brake fluid).

How dangerous are these substances to human health? In Los Angeles County a study concluded that the danger is insignificant. At two landfills, technicians sorted through sixty truckloads of solid wastes, including materials from homes and businesses. They found several thousand containers that had once held substances that could be considered dangerous. Most, however, were empty or held minute amounts of the product. The hazardous materials made up .13%, by weight, of all refuse. That is 2.69 pounds of hazardous materials in a ton of refuse.

The Los Angeles study concluded that the vast amounts of nonhazardous wastes safely absorbed the dangerous stuff. This finding may not apply to regions

Some communities hold special roundups of hazardous house-
hold wastes in order to keep these substances out of landfills.

with abundant rain, where special monitoring wells
show hazardous chemicals in leachate. However, the
outflow of leachate can be blocked by installing a clay
barrier and a system of pumps. Getting a barrier in
place is rather easy before a new landfill is opened, and
is required by some states. Building a leachate barrier
is more difficult and costly at existing landfills, many
of which were once open dumps.

Besides leachate and litter, landfills produce gases
from decaying organic matter. About half of landfill
gas is methane, which is also the main ingredient of
the natural gas used for cooking, heating, and gener-
ating electricity. Within landfills, concentrations of
methane have ignited and exploded. Venting shafts
are sometimes installed to prevent this.

Like leachate, gases can also seep underground beyond a landfill's borders. Explosive levels have been
found in the basements of homes near landfills; this
situation caused an explosion in a Wisconsin home
and severely burned two people. On Long Island,
New York, and in Richmond, Virginia, landfill methane forced the temporary closing of several elemen-
tary schools and the evacuation of people from nearby
homes. In Seattle, Washington, a landfill was closed in
1983 because both methane and leachate were spreading underground beyond its boundaries. Spreading
through underground gravel beds, the methane
reached homes a mile from the landfill, causing eleven
families to evacuate.

Unlike other landfill by-products, however, methane can also be an asset. Piped from beneath the surface, treated in ways that improve its heating qualities,
it can be sold to nearby businesses. With most water
vapor and carbon dioxide removed from landfill gas,
the remaining methane can be pumped directly into
gas utility pipelines.

The most productive landfills are those where
plenty of organic matter has been dumped, but a deposit must be deep and large—a minimum of a million
tons of refuse—in order to yield substantial amounts
of the gas. Several successful methane recovery proj-
ects are located in California, where most landfill sites
are deep canyons.

In the mid-1980s more than thirty landfills in the

At Fresh Kills, methane gas is recovered from 60 to 80 feet below the surface, treated to remove impurities, then injected into a nearby gas pipeline.

United States had methane recovery systems operating or under construction. Methane recovery is not highly profitable, but it helps defray costs of operating a landfill. Eventually, after a landfill closes and more and more of its contents decay, the amount of gas declines, and the recovery system is shut down.

When a landfill closes, a final layer of soil at least two feet deep is spread over its surface. As years pass, the surface settles a little, even if wastes were well compacted. Some landfills settle unevenly because they contain some materials (household garbage) that decay much faster than others (tree stumps). Developers have built homes on landfill, only to have foundations and walls crack as the land settles beneath the houses. Buildings can be erected on landfills, but only

In New Jersey, the Hackensack Meadowlands Environment Center perches over a marsh and at the edge of a landfill. Once dumping ends, the landfill will be made into a park.

after the underground decay is virtually complete, or pilings to support the structures are driven through the fill to underlying bedrock. In New Jersey, piles were driven 145 feet deep to support an environmental center built on a former landfill in the Hackensack Meadowlands.

Closed landfills can be made into recreation areas: parks with amphitheaters, running tracks, picnic grounds, ball fields, golf courses, tennis courts, archery ranges, and even ski slopes. People ski and sled on Mount Trashmore in Virginia Beach, but lasting snow cover is rare there. South of Detroit, Michigan,

No ordinary ski slope, Michigan's Riverview Highlands provides recreation atop a great heap of garbage and soil.

looms another vertical solid-waste-disposal site, the Riverview Highlands Ski Resort. It too was once called Mount Trashmore.

Riverview Highlands has eight slopes, several lifts and tows, and a vertical drop of 150 feet, with a longest run of 1,100 feet. Refuse and soil added to the mountain by 1988 will create an expert slope with a vertical drop of 176 feet. Compared with natural mountains, Riverview Highlands is just a hill, but it looms large in the flat terrain of southeastern Michigan and is a popular ski area.

One of the greatest challenges in landfill reclamation lies in northeastern New Jersey, where hundreds of acres of dumps and landfills will be gradually changed into part of a 2,000-acre park. Plans call for campsites and riding trails as well as ball fields and picnic areas among the hills, valleys, and meadows that will be sculpted from huge trash heaps.

Part of the challenge lies in getting grass, shrubs, and trees to thrive on the surfaces of former landfills. Many early attempts across the United States failed, but now the special conditions of landfill surfaces are better understood. It is sometimes necessary to reduce methane concentrations in the soil in order for roots to survive. Also, the decay process produces heat, which rises toward the landfill surface. Temperatures are not usually high enough to harm root systems directly, but they dry the soil and thereby threaten plant survival.

Scientists in the United States are investigating different kinds of grasses, shrubs, and other plants to discover which do well on landfills. They sometimes gain useful information from abroad. In England earthworms are released in the soil of retired landfills to help improve the structure and stability of the soil. And sheep are allowed to graze in areas where grasses are well-established. In some British communities, solid-waste-disposal costs are reduced a bit by the sale of grazing rights to farmers.

Creating a sheep meadow or ski slope on top of a heap of garbage seems to be a modern equivalent of that ancient dare, to make a silk purse from a sow's ear.

FIVE
BEYOND LANDFILLS

In the mid-1970s, many cities were warned that their landfills would soon be loaded to capacity. A decade later most of those landfills were still accepting solid wastes. A landfill, it has been said, is like soft luggage: you can always squeeze a little more in.

Actually, landfills do have finite limits; a trash mountain can rise only so high on a given acreage before its slopes become too steep for trucks to climb. New sites must be found. But concern about leachate means that no new landfills will be built on Long Island, New York, where 2.6 million people rely on groundwater from wells for their water supply.

Elsewhere, public opposition sometimes keeps a private operator or public agency from opening a new landfill. Even if it will someday be green open space,

Many old landfills have reached or exceeded their capacity, and no one wants a new landfill in their neighborhood.

a landfill is not something people want in their neighborhood. Aside from blown litter, odors, and other landfill pollution, there is increased truck traffic and spillage on roads leading to the site. In rural areas, farmers sometimes oppose new landfills because they fear crop damage from gulls, starlings, and other birds. Most of all, people are opposed to taking the trash of outsiders. Philadelphia faced this grim fact in 1986, when a New Jersey landfill stopped taking much of its garbage. Lacking landfill space within its borders, Philadelphia began trucking some of its waste 350 miles, to Ohio.

Increasingly, solid-waste managers must find ways to stretch the life of existing landfills or find other ways to dispose of refuse. One solution is to reduce the volume of wastes to be buried by first removing materials that have market value. The smart way to do this is to separate the materials at their source—homes or businesses—*before* all materials have been jumbled and mashed together in garbage trucks. This approach has been successful in many communities and especially in Marin County, California, which lies north of San Francisco. Participation by the public is voluntary, but nearly 40% of residents put their glass, metal cans, newsprint, and garbage in separate containers. In the month of December 1982, the recyclable materials amounted to 640 tons of newspapers, 148 tons of glass, 20 tons of aluminum cans, and 36 tons of steel cans.

The collection and sale of these materials for recycling is not usually profitable for Marin County. Prices for scrap steel and paper fluctuate wildly. Over a span of about two years in the early 1980s, paper prices ranged from over $60 a ton to $7 a ton. (The county's collected newsprint is sold to Korea and other Asian countries to make new paper products.)

Many communities encourage residents to separate such materials as glass for recycling. This separation may become mandatory in areas where landfill space is especially limited.

The only consistently profitable materials are cans, pie plates, and other items made of aluminum. In fact, this metal's value enticed some people to make off with aluminum items set out by residents for collection trucks. This led Marin County to establish a law that makes stealing garbage a misdemeanor.

This recycling program diverts about 300 truckloads each month from the county's landfill. It reduces the total volume ordinarily reaching the landfill by about 6%, and thereby extends its life while the county government seeks alternatives to landfilling.

In 1983 a similar volunteer recycling program was launched in Minneapolis, Minnesota, where solid-waste-disposal costs had doubled in four years and were expected to double again by 1990. The city's long-range goal was to collect 32,500 tons of news-print, cans, and other salable materials each year—achieving a 25% reduction from the wastes Minneapolis collected before the program began. By 1985 the city's effort was the nation's largest voluntary waste-separation project, with between 20% and 25% of its population participating. The volume of waste reaching landfills was reduced by about 7%, far from the city's goal, and Minneapolis launched a publicity campaign to promote participation.

Reliance on voluntary recycling efforts may not be enough in some regions—the state of New Jersey, for example. Its residents produce 13.5 million tons of solid wastes each year, with 92% of this volume deposited in sixteen landfills. By 1985, all these landfills were more than 25% beyond their capacity. The New Jersey Department of Environmental Protection devised a plan for statewide mandatory recycling, in which every homeowner or apartment dweller would have to separate wastes into several categories before collection. The New Jersey legislature seemed likely to enact a mandatory refuse separation law in 1986.

Long before such recycling programs were established, some cities reduced their refuse volume by incineration. But more stringent air-pollution laws have made refuse burning costly. Cities have had to close old incinerators or install "scrubbers" that reduce harmful smokestack emissions.

In a few cities, such as Cincinnati, Ohio, old inciner-

The great amounts of cardboard and paper in solid wastes hold high energy value that can be converted into steam and electricity.

ators are being rebuilt as resource recovery plants. These facilities are also called waste-to-energy plants. Cities in densely populated Europe pioneered in the process of using solid waste as fuel to produce steam and electricity. Beginning in the 1970s, as landfills became more jam-packed in the United States, many cities began to investigate ways to get energy, metals, and other resources from their solid wastes.

The idea of converting troublesome trash to cash was appealing. Newspapers and other media gave glowing reports of the riches in solid wastes, or "urban ore," as some called it. Wildly enthusiastic claims were made about the ease and economics of resource recovery. Some cities and corporations spent many millions of dollars to build elaborate plants that failed to meet expectations, or simply failed to work. Several major corporations ventured into this field, then withdrew when the difficulties became clear.

In 1979, for example, a resource recovery plant opened in Bridgeport, Connecticut. It was designed to turn 1,800 tons of garbage a day into "refuse-derived fuel," a powdery material that could be mixed with oil to generate electricity. The troubled plant shut down after a year and a half of operation, having burned less than a month's supply of garbage in that time. The Bridgeport plant produced one memorable product— an odor one state environmental inspector called "bad enough to gag a maggot."

A similar plant was built in Hempstead, Long Island, New York, at a cost of about $135 million. Foul smells were a problem there too, reportedly causing people in nearby parking lots to vomit. But it was the presence of high levels of the toxic chemical dioxin in the plant's gaseous emissions that caused it to be shut down in 1979. More than $10 million was spent in an unsuccessful effort to remedy the situation. By the early 1990s the plant will be converted to a simpler process that burns refuse to produce electricity. Meanwhile, Hempstead is short of landfill space and must pay $67 a ton to dispose of 720 tons a day at a landfill that is a hundred miles away.

Another troubled waste-to-energy plant was built in Akron, Ohio. Opened in 1979, the waste-burning plant worked poorly and had to be closed and redesigned. Operating once more, in the fall of 1983 the plant sustained ten different explosions. Exploding aerosol cans caused minor damage, but several explosions caused by plastic residues, cosmetic wastes, and gases from decaying garbage required more than a million dollars to repair. Then in December 1984 the plant accepted a truckload of industrial wastes from New Jersey. The shippers claimed that the contents were sawdust and waste oil, but they also included paint residues and solvents. These wastes caused fiery explosions that killed three people and injured seven others. After more than $2.5 million in repairs the plant resumed operation in 1985, with a new policy of accepting only household garbage.

Not all plants that produce refuse-derived fuel have been as troubled as those in Bridgeport, Hempstead, and Akron. The same general type of plant has worked fairly well in Milwaukee and New Orleans. Metals and other noncombustible materials are removed and the remaining refuse is shredded into fuel. The shredding process, however, makes explosions almost inevitable. A partly full tank of propane gas or even a container of shellac can pass unnoticed by inspectors and explode as powerful shredders pulverize the wastes. Engineers have learned that it is best to control such explosions by using vents rather than trying to contain them.

Plants that produce refuse-derived fuel are more complex than those that simply burn garbage to produce energy. As a general rule, the more complicated a resource recovery plant is, the more frequently it breaks down. An exception is a plant in Florida, where a complex process involving several sorting devices and eighty different conveyor belts produces refuse-derived fuel from which electricity is generated. The plant was built privately by Resources Recovery, Inc., for $165 million and was later purchased by Dade County.

Thirteen communities in the Miami area and more than fifty private trash-collecting firms bring wastes to the plant. Most household garbage is dumped into a "tipping area" or pit capable of holding 6,000 tons. Cranes bite refuse from the pit and drop it onto conveyors that carry it into a forty-five-foot-long sorting device called a trommel. It shakes the refuse. Small objects fall through 2½-inch holes onto another conveyor belt. (Some sand, soil, and glass is also removed by this process.) Large or small, all objects from the trommel are conveyed to twenty-foot-wide blenders, called hydrapulpers.

Water is added, creating a slurry, or watery mixture. The whole mess is stirred rapidly. Centrifugal force carries heavy objects, including metals, to the container's walls, where they are scooped off by automatically moving buckets. The metals pass over a magnet so that steel and iron (ferrous metals) can be separated from other metals.

From the hydrapulpers the slurry of wastes goes

through further processes that remove small bits of noncombustible material and squeeze water from the remainder. (Water in the plant is used over and over again.) The wastes are then conveyed to the boilers and burned to generate electricity.

Another stream of wastes begins at a second tipping area, which receives non-household waste. This trash includes wood and other construction debris, tree limbs, and furniture. Appliances made of steel are sorted out for sale as scrap metal. The rest is loaded onto a conveyor, which carries it to two huge shredding machines powered by a 1,250-horsepower engine.

Workers watch the trash as it is carried along, ready to remove such objects as auto engines, which foul the shredders, and explosive substances. The Dade County plant was designed and built so that explosions during the shredding process would cause no harm.

After ferrous metals are removed from the shredded trash, the trash is burned in boilers. From all its refuse-derived fuel, the plant produces steam that generates about fifty megawatts of electricity a day— equal to the amount used by 50,000 to 60,000 homes.

Trucks enter a modern mass-burning resource-recovery plant (top). Inside, a crane grabs wastes (center) and deposits them in a chamber where temperatures may exceed 1,800 degrees Fahrenheit (bottom). The heat is used to generate electricity.

The Dade County plant is fortunate in having nearby markets for nearly everything it produces—metals, glass, and even the ash from its boilers. The metals recovered at the Dade County plant are clean and more readily sold than the contaminated metals that are recovered from the ashes of mass-burning plants.

Another resource recovered is money. Twenty-five thousand dollars in coins were recovered in the plant's first six months of operation. (Presumably much larger amounts of paper money were burned.) Over-all, the Dade County plant gets about 30% of its income from sale of by-products and 70% from sale of electricity. Its revenue usually equals its operating costs.

This resource-recovery plant produces as much as 160 tons of residue daily. Most of the ash is sold to local concrete product manufacturers, who use it in making concrete blocks and in highway construction. After sale of the ashes only about twenty tons of residue must be buried daily in a landfill adjacent to the plant. This gives the Dade County facility a clear advantage over mass-burning plants, which burn from 60% to 80% by weight of the solid wastes they take in. (The volume is reduced much more than the weight.)

A mass-burning plant that takes in 3,000 tons of trash a day may produce 1,000 tons of ashes. Finding markets for the residue is difficult, so mass-burning plants need considerable landfill space for their left-overs. If New York City succeeds in its plan to burn all of its wastes in ten new mass-burning resource-recovery plants, it will still need to find landfill space for 1.6 million tons of ash each year.

Mass-burning plants are cheaper to build and simpler to operate than those that produce refuse-derived fuel. Mass burning to produce steam and electricity is common in European cities, and Chicago and Nashville also have mass burners. One of the most successful of these plants is in Saugus, Massachusetts, north of Boston. It opened in 1976 and burns up to 1,500 tons of trash a day from eighteen communities. Solid wastes are dumped into a storage pit, then lifted out by a crane and deposited onto a grate on which the refuse is burned. The trash is not sorted or shredded. It burns under pressure at high temperatures (1,800 degrees Fahrenheit). Steam from the boilers is piped to a nearby jet-engine manufacturing plant. Beginning in 1985, some was used to produced electricity, which was then sold to the New England Electric Company.

Dozens of cities and counties are investigating ways to deal with their solid wastes. The resource-recovery business is "taking off like a rocket," according to an industry official. A hundred new plants may be built by the year 2000, it is predicted, with a third of the nation's garbage burned to produce electricity. This concerns some environmentalists, who believe that the smokestack emissions from resource recovery plants may contain hazardous amounts of pollutants and need further investigation. They also favor recycling as much waste material as possible before refuse is burned.

Trouble may lie ahead for those who currently recover and sell metals and other recyclable materials, and for those who hope to do so in the future. Will there be markets for these materials as more and more communities separate them from other solid wastes? The demand for recyclable materials has always varied, and continues to change. The need for scrap glass, for example, has declined as more beverages are bottled in plastic. Unless markets for recyclable materials expand, a lot of cities may have no buyers for their ever-growing piles of neatly sorted trash. They may have to pay scrap dealers to take recyclable materials.

There is also potential conflict between proponents of recycling and of waste-to-energy plants. Consider paper, for example. Paper recycling is a big business in the United States. There are 1,500 wastepaper dealers, who supply more than 200 paper and paperboard mills that rely entirely on wastepaper as raw material. Another 500 mills use some wastepaper. In all, about 18 million tons of paper are recycled each year. So wastepaper dealers want to encourage paper recycling in order to maintain or increase their supplies.

On the other hand, if one's goal is to burn solid wastes and convert some of its energy value to electricity, one wants paper products left in. Newspapers, cardboard, and other paper products often make up

Increased use of plastic for beverage containers has reduced the demand for scrap glass.

half of all residential solid waste and provide much of its energy value. Thus, recycling of paper can be seen as a threat to the supply of waste that resource recovery plants need in order to produce electricity.

In Akron, Ohio, this need led to conflict between the city and paper-recycling companies. The city government enacted a "flow-control" law to ensure an uninterrupted flow of paper and other trash to its waste-to-energy plant. It laid claim to any solid waste as soon as it was discarded within the city limits. In effect, Akron outlawed recycling. On a large scale, a law like this might increase national demand for wood pulp, with more and more trees cut down to be used just once for paper, then burned for energy.

Paper recyclers challenged Akron in court, claiming that the flow-control law restrained trade. They argued that paper collectors should be free to take wastepaper wherever they want. The court, however, supported Akron's attempt to gain legal control of the flow of wastes produced by its residents.

A fight over control of refuse may seem bizarre, but it is a symptom of the great changes sweeping through the field of solid-waste management. The changes bring difficult questions: What sort of resource recovery plant is best? Will the waste gases from such plants be a threat to health? Answers to such questions may not be known for many years, and people who try to manage solid wastes do not feel that they can wait for certainty.

Something must be done. Dumps and landfills, so cheap and easy to run a few decades ago, have become much more costly and troublesome. Space is running out. New landfill sites, when they can be found, are long, expensive hauls for a city's garbage trucks.

The next stage of dealing with human trash will be well under way by the turn of the century. Millions of people will be obliged by law to separate recyclable materials from the rest of their refuse. In many cities, all remaining waste will go to resource-recovery plants. Numerous landfills will no longer receive loads of fresh garbage, except when a plant breaks down or can no longer absorb all of a community's solid wastes.

Many dumps and landfills will close forever. Long into the next century, however, some will persist in

Hundreds of open dumps and landfills have been closed, and many others will eventually be replaced by resource-recovery plants.

rural areas and small towns. There will still be dumping grounds where gulls can find something to eat, and where people can bring their refuse, pause to chat, and look around for something of value to take home.

FURTHER READING

Barry, Patrick. "Cities Rush to Recycle." *Sierra*, November–December 1985, pp. 32–35.

Blokpoel, Hans. *Gull Problems in Ontario.* Ontario Information Leaflet. Ottawa: Canadian Wildlife Service, 1983.

Burger, Joanna. "Feeding Competition Between Laughing Gulls and Herring Gulls at a Sanitary Landfill." *Condor*, volume 83 (1981), pp. 328–335.

Burger, Joanna, and Gochfeld, Michael. "Behavior of Nine Avian Species at a Florida Garbage Dump." *Colonial Waterbirds*, volume 6 (1983), pp. 54–63.

Earley, Kathleen. "The Archeology of Tucson." *The Sciences*, December 1974, pp. 12–14.

Forsythe, Dennis. "Gulls, Solid Waste Disposal, and the Bird-Aircraft Strike Hazard." Proceedings of conference

"Biological Aspects of the Bird-Aircraft Collision Problem," 1974, pp. 17–25 (unpublished).

Glysson, Eugene, et al. *The Problem of Solid-Waste Disposal.* Ann Arbor, Michigan: College of Engineering, 1972.

Harrison, Michael, et al., editors. *Wildlife Hazards to Aircraft Conference and Training Workshop.* Washington, D.C.: Department of Transportation, 1984 (available from National Technical Information Service, Springfield, Virginia 22161).

Hertel, Holly. "The Role of Social Niche in Juvenile Wolves: Puppyhood to Independence." M.S. thesis, University of Minnesota, 1984.

Johnson, Bruce. "Methane Gas, Leachate Create Landfill Problems." *World Wastes,* December 1983, pp. 10–11.

Koppel, Tom. "Indian Shell Middens." *Oceans,* May 1985, pp. 18–22.

Mathias, Sandra. "Discouraging Seagulls: The Los Angeles Approach." *Waste Age,* November 1984, pp. 176, 161.

Melosi, Martin. *Garbage in the Cities: Refuse, Reform, and the Environment.* College Station, Texas: Texas A&M Press, 1981.

Nelson, Luann. "Dade Plant Running at Full Capacity." *World Wastes,* May 1983, pp. 10–11, 44–45.

Noble, Vergil, Jr. "Excavating Fort Ouiatenon, a French Fur Trading Post." *Archaeology,* March–April 1982, pp. 71–73.

O'Connor, John. "Landfill Methane Recovery: Can It Be Profitable?" *American City and County,* March 1982, pp. 52–54.

Shimell, Pamela. "Plant Life Restores Waste Disposal Sites." *World Wastes*, July 1983, pp. 26–27, 48.

Stegner, Wallace. *Wolf Willow*. New York: Viking, 1962 (the essay "The Dump Ground" appears on pages 31–36).

Steinhart, Peter. "Down in the Dumps." *Audubon*, May 1986, pp. 102–109.

White, Peter. "The Fascinating World of Trash." *National Geographic*, April 1983, pp. 424–457.

Wiley, John, Jr. "Polar Bear Capital of the World." *Smithsonian*, March 1986, pp. 40–53.

INDEX

Page numbers in *italics* refer to illustrations